The Shining Stars

GREEK LEGENDS OF THE ZODIAC

by Ghislaine Vautier
adapted by Kenneth McLeish

illustrated by Jacqueline Bezençon

CAMBRIDGE UNIVERSITY PRESS
Cambridge
New York   Port Chester
Melbourne   Sydney

PEOPLE
IN THE STORIES

Nowadays, in books and films and on television, there are many exciting stories about stars and the planets of outer space. Three thousand years ago, the ancient Greeks had their kind of space fiction too. They looked up at the stars, and wondered how they came to be where they were and make the shapes they made.

The stories in this book are Greek legends connected with each of the twelve star-signs. At the end of the book are star-maps, to help you find each of the constellations in the night sky. If you want to read more myths and legends of ancient Greece, or more about astronomy (the study of the stars), your school or local library will have plenty of books to help.

Adonis (a-DOH-niss). A beautiful young man, son of the princess Myrrha. Before he was born, his mother angered Aphrodite and was changed into a sweet-smelling balsam tree. When the tree split open, baby Adonis was found inside.

Aeëtes (ai-EE-tees). King of Colchis near the Black Sea. He was made guardian of the Golden Fleece.

Amalthea (a-mal-THAY-a). A mountain nymph in the shape of a she-goat, who fed the baby Zeus on her milk.

Aphrodite (a-fro-DIE-tee). Goddess of love and beauty. She was born from the foam of the sea, and her name means "foam-born".

Artemis (AR-te-miss). Daughter of Zeus, goddess of hunting and the protector of all growing creatures.

Cheiron (KAY-ron). Son of Kronos and half-brother of Zeus. King of the centaurs, creatures half horse half man.

Demeter (dee-MEE-ter). Sister of Zeus and mother of Persephone. Goddess of the earth and of all growing plants.

Eros (e-ROHS or EE-ross). Son of Aphrodite and god of love. A mischievous boy whose arrows caused not death but the pain of instant love. He is also often known as Cupid.

Europa (yoo-ROH-pa). A pretty girl carried away by the sacred bull of Zeus. She later gave her name to the continent of Europe.

Ganymede (GAN-i-meed). A Trojan shepherd who became cup-bearer of the gods.

Hades (HAY-dees). Zeus' brother, king of the Underworld. The people of his dark kingdom were the souls of the dead, as countless as leaves at the turn of the year.

Helios (HEE-li-oss). The sun-god.

Helle (HEL-le). Sister of Phrixos.

Hera (HEE-ra). Daughter of Kronos and queen of heaven. Goddess of marriages. She was often fierce and cruel to mortals she disliked.

Herakles (HER-a-klees). Son of Zeus and a mortal mother, Alkmene. He was a powerful fighter, and is the hero of many exciting adventures.

Hermes (HER-mees). Zeus' son, the messenger of the gods.

Hydra (HY-dra). A snake-monster, daughter of Typhon. Her breath and blood were deadly poison.

Iolaos (ee-o-LA-oss). Nephew of Herakles, and his helper on many of his adventures.

Kastor (KASS-tor). Son of Zeus, twin brother of Pollux, a famous athlete and warrior.

Kronos (KRO-noss). Zeus' father and first ruler of the universe. His other children included Hades, Poseidon, Hera and Demeter.

Melissa (mel-ISS-a). Mountain nymph who looked after baby Zeus. Her name means "honey".

Olympos (o-LIM-poss). A high mountain, on the peaks of which the gods had their kingdom.

Orion (o-RI-on). A skilful hunter.

Persephone (per-SEF-o-nee). Demeter's daughter, queen of the Underworld.

Phrixos (FRIX-oss). Helle's brother, saved from sacrifice by the ram of Zeus, whose golden fleece he later gave to his foster-father Aeëtes.

Pollux (POL-lux). Twin brother of Kastor. His name is also given as Polydeukes.

Poseidon (pos-AY-don). Zeus' brother, king of the sea, of horses and of earthquakes.

Rhea (REE-a). Wife of Kronos, and mother of Zeus, Poseidon, Hades, Hera and Demeter.

Selene (sel-EE-nee). Moon-goddess, sister of Helios.

Themis (THE-miss). Goddess of wisdom and common sense.

Typhon (TY-phon). A hideous monster, son of Earth and father of Hydra.

Zeus (z-YOO-ss). The most powerful god in Olympos, ruler of gods and men. He was the sky-god, and when he was angry he used to hurl thunderbolts and lightning-shafts. He often disguised himself (as an eagle, a bull, or a mortal man) and went down to earth in search of adventure.

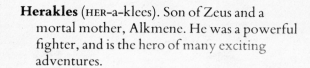

THE HORN OF PLENTY

Capricorn

In Crete, in a grassy field on the slopes of Mount Ida, the spirit warriors were exercising. They were practising fighting with swords and spears. At the edge of the field a she-goat called Amalthea quietly cropped the grass.

A young girl, Melissa, came up with bowls of yellow honey. "Look, Amalthea," she said. "Honey for the warriors' breakfast."

All at once the air went still, as if every creature on the mountain was holding its breath, awed by the coming of an immortal goddess: Rhea, queen of heaven, herself. In her arms she carried a newborn baby wrapped in a shawl.

Melissa curtseyed to the queen. To her surprise, Rhea suddenly burst into tears and thrust the baby into her arms. "Oh Melissa," she sobbed, "please help my newborn son! His name is Zeus. His father, King Kronos, is afraid that one of his sons will drive him out of his kingdom and seize the throne. So whenever a new baby is born, he snatches it and eats it alive. Please help me save Zeus' life!"

Melissa smiled down at baby Zeus. "Don't worry, my lady," she said to Rhea. "I'll keep him safe for you."

Rhea took a large stone and wrapped it in Zeus' shawl. She carried it back to heaven, and Kronos, thinking it was his baby, opened his huge mouth

and gulped it down. On earth, Melissa laid the real Zeus in a golden cradle. Every day the she-goat Amalthea fed him on her milk. The warriors danced and shouted, and their noise drowned the baby's crying or laughing. So Kronos never knew that his son was still alive.

As the boy grew older, he often wrestled with Amalthea, holding her by the horns and trying to throw her to the ground. One day, in the middle of such a wrestling match, Zeus heard a sudden snap. One of Amalthea's horns had come off in his hand. "It's a sign," he said to himself. "The time has come for me to punish my father and rescue my swallowed-up brothers and sisters."

He took the horn to Melissa. "Look after it," he said. "It's a magic Horn of Plenty. It will provide food and drink for you forever. Now I must go; but one day I'll call Amalthea to join me in heaven."

For many years there were battles in heaven as Zeus fought his cruel father Kronos. On earth, on the slopes of Mount Ida, life went on peacefully as before. Then one day, from a clear sky, Amalthea heard Zeus' voice calling her. "Amalthea, come! Take your place in heaven."

Still, today, the she-goat Amalthea, nursemaid of Zeus, gambols in the meadows of the sky, a constellation of stars for evermore.

Aquarius

The gods lived carefree, happy lives. All day they galloped their chariots in heaven, along the wide road of the Milky Way. At night they sat feasting in marble palaces on Mount Olympos. Their food was called ambrosia. It was a delicious kind of cake, and it made anyone who ate it immortal – that is, able to live forever. Their drink was a mixture of fruit juices and honey, called nectar.

Because eating ambrosia made people immortal, the gods kept it for themselves. Only a very few mortals were allowed to taste it – and when they did, they became immortal too, and went to live with the gods in heaven.

One of these mortals was called Ganymede. He was a shepherd boy from Troy, and he was the gods' favourite, one of the gentlest and most beautiful mortals they had ever seen. One evening he was playing with his dog, Argos, in a field beside a quiet stream. Soon it would be sunset, time to drive the sheep home for the night. But now they were feeding peacefully at the edge of a grove of olive trees. Ganymede had plaited Argos a collar of olive-twigs. He was throwing sticks for Argos to fetch.

"Here, boy! Fetch! There's a good boy!" he called. Argos ran for the sticks, barking eagerly. The scent of flowers and grass rose in the cool evening air. An owl had woken up, and was hooting in the shadows beside the stream.

"Come on then, Argos," said Ganymede at last. "Time to go home."

He lifted his shepherd's pipe to call the sheep. But there was a sudden whirr of wings, a dark shadow loomed overhead, and a gigantic eagle flew down and perched beside the flock.

"Argos! Attack!" shouted Ganymede. But instead of chasing off the eagle, Argos crouched down in front of it, flattening his ears and thumping his tail on the ground. Ganymede stood still in astonishment.

He was even more astonished when the eagle opened its beak and spoke. "Come here, Ganymede. Don't be afraid. I'm Zeus' eagle, and my master has sent me to carry you to Olympos. Because of your gentleness and beauty, you will become an immortal, the cupbearer of the gods."

"But my lord . . . the sheep . . ." stammered Ganymede. "How will they get safely home?"

"Argos will lead them," said the eagle. "Take this feather and fasten it with your pipe in Argos' collar. Your parents will recognise them, and know that you are safe with the gods in heaven."

So saying, he plucked a feather from his huge wing. Ganymede fastened it, with his pipe, in Argos' collar. Argos licked his hand, and looked up for the last time into his master's eyes. Then he rounded up the sheep and began to drive them home.

The eagle bent its neck, and settled Ganymede carefully on its back between its huge wings. Then, silently, majestically, it soared up into the darkness of the evening sky.

Down below, on the pathway beside the stream, the sheepbells tinkled as the flock moved off. Argos looked up. He barked with joy to see his master soaring above him: Ganymede, cupbearer of the gods, like a glittering new constellation in the sky.

DRAGON RESCUE

Pisces

The goddess Aphrodite was playing marbles with her son Eros. Instead of marbles they were using whole walnuts. They were trying to teach their pet dove to push the marbles and join in the game.

"Look, look, she's pushing it!" shouted Eros excitedly.

The dove pushed Aphrodite's walnut out of the way, then fluttered up and perched on a branch to watch the game. Now it was Eros' turn. He crooked finger and thumb, flicked his walnut, and sent Aphrodite's spinning out of the area.

"I've won! I've won!" he cried.

"Very good," smiled Aphrodite.

"Now, run and play. I want to sit in the shade and rest."

"I'll go into the wood, and hunt with my new bow and arrows."

"All right, but be careful. They're dangerous toys," said Aphrodite. Eros ran off into the wood, and she stretched out on the soft grass. The cooing of the dove, and the rippling of a tiny stream nearby, were like a lullaby in her ears. Butterflies hovered around her, watching as she slept.

Then there was a scream of fear, and the butterflies fluttered away in alarm. Aphrodite jumped up, as Eros came running terrified from the wood.

"Run!" he shouted. "A monster! Run and hide!"

"What is it?"

"It has a dragon's head and red, fiery eyes. Instead of arms and legs it has hundreds of coiling snakes. It was hiding, waiting in the wood."

"Typhon! The gods' enemy!"
"It's coming! It wants to kill us!"
"Run, Eros, run!"

Panting and terrified, Aphrodite and Eros ran for their lives. Behind them they could near the crashing of branches as Typhon slithered through the wood. Animals and birds hurtled past them, desperate for safety.

All at once, they stopped short. They had run the wrong way, and come to the seashore. They were trapped: endless sea in front, and Typhon coming up fast behind.

"We're lost, Eros," said Aphrodite. "Try to be brave."

They stood trembling, waiting for Typhon to come and eat them alive. The panting and slithering came nearer and nearer. Then, in the very nick of time, a pair of sleek black dolphins appeared in the waves in front of them. Beside them, as they leapt and gambolled through the water, Poseidon god of the sea rose up, trident in hand.

"Climb on their backs," he said. "They'll save you. Typhon won't dare to follow them out to sea."

When Typhon came snorting and writhing down to the shore, Aphrodite and Eros were safe on the dolphins' backs. Furious, helpless, the monster shook his dragon fists and roared. But there was nothing he could do. He lifted his head to hiss at Zeus – and there he saw a new constellation in the dolphins' shape, winking and gleaming in the sky above his head.

THE GOLDEN FLEECE

Aries

The palace of Zeus, king of gods and men, stands high on the peaks of Mount Olympos. A curtain of mist hides it from the eyes of mortal men. But Zeus looks down, and sees everything men do on earth.

One day Zeus looked down towards the temple at Delphi. What he saw made him frown with anger. A group of mortals was preparing a terrible sacrifice. On one side three priests held two terrified children, Phrixos and his sister Helle; on the other side stood a wicked king and his queen, the children's cruel stepmother. They were going to burn the children alive as a sacrifice to Zeus.

Zeus called to his pet ram. Instead of white wool, its fleece was made of curling yellow gold. "Hurry," he said. "Go down and rescue them."

Just as the priests lifted their knives to begin the sacrifice, there was a flash of lightning above their heads, and a golden cloud appeared before them. In the middle was the ram. "Climb on to my back," it said to the children. "Climb on. Hurry!"

Phrixos and Helle climbed up and took tight hold of the ram's soft golden fleece. The ram leapt into the sky, leaving the priests and the cruel king and queen far below.

For hours the ram soared across the sky. It passed over cloud-capped mountains, grey-blue seas, flat farmlands and villages with pencils of smoke rising from people's cooking fires below. Still holding tight, soothed by the soft breeze, Phrixos and Helle fell fast asleep.

At last, as the sun was setting, the ram came to earth with a little hop and bump. Phrixos woke up. "Where are we?" he asked sleepily.

"In Colchis, in a safe country," said the ram. "Here you'll grow up as the foster-son of King Aeëtes."

"Where's Helle?" said Phrixos in alarm. "She's fallen off! She's drowned!"

"No," said the ram. "Not drowned. While you were asleep. Poseidon lord of the sea took her to serve him in his palace under the sea."

Phrixos' eyes filled with tears. "Will I never see her again?"

"You must be brave and serve Zeus, just as she now serves Poseidon. Take your knife and sacrifice me. Then carry my golden fleece to your new father, King Aeëtes."

"But – "

"Do as Zeus commands!"

Tearfully Phrixos sacrificed the ram and gathered its fleece in his arms. Then he set off towards Aeëtes' palace. His heart was sad because Zeus had made him kill the ram which had saved his life.

Then he looked up at the starry sky, and understood. The ram's fleece was left on earth as a sign of Zeus' kindness to men. But the golden ram itself now gambolled in the sky, a constellation of bright stars that guided his steps as he went joyfully on his way.

BEYOND THE HORIZON

Taurus

As well as the mainland of Greece, there are hundreds of islands. Some are large, but many are tiny, and only a handful of people live on them. Their news and entertainment come by boat, brought by travellers from other islands and other parts of Greece.

Once a travelling entertainer called Oknos sailed round the islands in a small boat. Everywhere he went the islanders flocked to see him. He was a juggler and an acrobat, and he also owned two performing animals, a monkey and a dancing pig.

One day Oknos gave a show to some girls on the beach of a small island. One of the girls was called Europa. She and her friends laughed with delight at the antics of Simos the monkey and Krokon the pig. They listened round-eyed to Oknos' tales of the world outside their island, of the strange sights and wonderful adventures that happened "just beyond the horizon".

At last Oknos packed away his stilts, his juggling-clubs and his magic tricks, and whistled to the animals to climb into the boat. The show was done.

The girls gathered to watch him go. "Goodbye, Oknos," they called. "Where are you sailing now?"

"Beyond the horizon."

"Goodbye! Goodbye!"

They went on waving and calling until the little boat was out of sight. Then, laughing and shouting, they went to play ball in a field beside the beach. Only Europa stayed by herself. She stood on the shore, gazing out over the blue sea.

"Oh Zeus," she sighed, "If only I could travel beyond the horizon, like Oknos, and have all the wonderful adventures he told us about. Oh Zeus, please answer my prayer."

There was no answer but the sigh of the wind and the chuckling of waves on the pebbly beach. Sadly she went to play with the other girls.

At the edge of the field she found a large, snow-white bull. Its horns were twisted like crescent moons. Bulls are usually fierce and dangerous; but this one was so gentle that the girls were able to stroke it, tickle its ears and garland its horns with daisy-chains.

As Europa came up, the bull bent its front legs and knelt down before her. It looked at her with gentle eyes and lowed softly. She offered it a handful of clover and then, very carefully, climbed onto its back. At once it stood up and moved off towards the beach. Europa took hold of its horns and held on tight.

When the bull reached the beach it plunged straight into the sea and began to swim. Faster and faster it went, and Europa dug her heels into its sides to encourage it. "On you go!" she said. "Carry me as far as you can, beyond the horizon!"

On the bull swam. It passed Oknos and his animals, in their sailing-boat. They waved. At last, long after sunset, the bull came to the island of Crete and splashed ashore on a sandy beach. Once again it knelt, and Europa climbed down from its back. There, on the shore, Zeus himself stood waiting. He held out his hands and smiled.

"Welcome, Europa," he said. "Your prayer has been answered. You have sailed beyond the horizon, and your wonderful adventure has just begun."

WILL O' THE WISPS

Gemini

Up above, in the sunlit meadows of Olympos, Zeus' twin sons Kastor and Pollux were practising sports. They wrestled, boxed, ran, jumped and threw the javelin. Each was his brother's best friend and fiercest rival. Kastor was better at some sports, Pollux better at others; but at most they were evenly matched. The whole of Olympos rang with their shouts as they ran and jumped.

Down below on earth, the sky was black with clouds and the sea churned and heaved in a ferocious storm. In the middle of the dark water a small boat tossed helplessly. The moon and stars were blotted out by clouds; the boat's sail flapped torn and useless against the mast; the lone sailor, a boy called Iphis, struggled to row his boat through the pitch darkness to safety on the shore. His cargo of oil-jars rolled and bumped as waves battered his boat; rain stung his face, and cold sea-water slopped and rolled in the bottom of the boat.

All at once the boat lurched violently as a huge wave smashed into its side. The oars splintered in Iphis' hands and were snatched away into the darkness. He put his head in his hands and groaned. "What hope is there of safety now?" he thought. "If only I could see a little in this darkness, I could find a safe place to drop anchor and sleep till the storm blows over. But it's pitch-black, and all I can do is wait till the waves smash my boat to pieces on the rocks."

The wind howled, and the sea roared and beat on the boat. Iphis fell on his knees and lifted his hands to pray. "Oh Zeus, help me! Take pity on me and send me light!"

At once, like twin rays of hope in the darkness, a pair of lights appeared and hovered at the tip of the mast. Their borders glowed warm and golden; in the centre they gleamed with a pale, milk-white brightness. They danced and flickered round the mast-tip, moving like boxers or athletes running on the spot. They gave just enough light for Iphis to see a way between the rocks. He found a safe place where the sea-bottom was sandy, and dropped anchor for the night. He fell on his knees again and gave thanks to Zeus. Then, exhausted, he lay back in the boat and fell asleep.

Back on Olympos, Kastor and Pollux yawned and stretched. "Come on, brother," said Kastor. "We need some sleep as well. The hardest sport of all is helping men, and being a will o' the wisp."

Pollux said nothing. He was fast asleep.

MONSTERS

Cancer

In a swamp beside a river, at the foot of a seven-branched plane tree, was the lair of a hideous monster called Hydra. It had a dragon's body and nine snaky heads, each with poison-fangs and a darting, flickering tongue. Its breath was so poisonous that it choked anyone who tried to cross the swamp. Hydra fed on mortal men: the muddy ground round its lair was littered with the bones of its victims. There was no way of killing it: every time a head was sliced off, another grew at once in its place, ever fiercer than before.

Hydra was protected by Hera, queen of heaven. She hated a mortal man, Herakles, the strongest and bravest fighter there had ever been. She was waiting for the day when Hydra would fight him and kill him. To help Hydra, she had a giant crab with razor-sharp pincers. Its job was to come up behind Herakles and hold him while Hydra finished him.

At last the day of the contest came. Herakles and his friend Iolaos were travelling through that part of Greece, and their way led straight to Hydra's lair. It was night. Herakles carried his bow and arrows, and Iolaos held a blazing pine-torch to light the way.

Suddenly, ahead of them in the darkness, they saw the gleam of eyes: eighteen snake's-eyes, glittering green with evil. Hydra's monstrous shape reared up and blocked their way. "Sss!" it hissed, its nine heads talking as one. "No mortal passes here. Stay here and die!"

But the gods had warned Herakles and told him what to do. Quickly he shot an arrow through the nearest head. Then, in the instant it was wounded, Iolaos scorched the stump with his blazing torch, and so stopped another head growing there.

One by one they dealt with the heads. The ground was slippery and slimy with Hydra's blood, and they were almost choked with its poison-breath. But they struggled on until there was only one head left.

Then, just as Herakles was about to shoot his last arrow, Hera's crab ran sideways out of the swamp and fastened its pincers round his ankle. It thought he was unarmed; but it was wrong. Furious with pain and anger, he lifted his other foot and stamped on its shell, crushing it to death with a single blow.

So Hera's plan failed. Hydra was killed, and Herakles lived to fight many more monsters. And the crab was taken into the sky as a constellation of stars, in memory of the battle in which it played such a tiny and such a useless part.

THE NEMEAN LION

Leo

A savage lion lived on the moon, in a cave of grey rock. At night it slept huddled in a corner of the cave for warmth. By day it hunted. But there was no food on the barren moon, and the lion grew ever hungrier and fiercer. At last it could bear its hunger no longer. It lay in wait, until the moon-goddess Selene galloped past in her chariot. Then it sprang out and pounced on one of her chariot-horses.

Just in time, Selene flicked the horses with her whip and the moon-chariot flashed past out of range. The lion missed its footing and plunged down through the sky like a shooting-star. It landed on earth, in Nemea in Greece. Like all cats, it fell on its feet, and so was unharmed. Flicking its tail, it looked round with angry yellow eyes, still ravenous for food. It saw an olive tree, a cave, and a boy playing.

They cut down the tree and made a huge, knotted club. Just as they finished, the lion came out. At once Herakles lifted the club and hit it – not on the head, but on the end of its nose. Startled, the lion ran whimpering and sneezing back into its cave. Herakles ran in after it.

Outside, the farmer listened in terror to the sounds of a huge struggle. Then there was silence. Sure that the lion had won, the old man was sadly setting off for home when Herakles came out of the cave, wearing the lion's skin as a cloak and its head as a helmet. He had strangled it to death with his bare hands, and used its own razor-claws to cut the skin. As the farmer watched, amazed, the voice of Zeus himself rang out from the clear sky.

"Well done, Herakles! I shall sow lion-stars in the sky in honour of this victory."

With one bound the lion fell on the boy, dragged him to the cave and finished him off. From now on it would feast on human prey.

Years later, the hero Herakles was travelling through Nemea when he found the boy's father sitting by the tree, still weeping for his son.

"Help me cut down this tree and make a club," said Herakles. "I'll deal with the lion for you."

"It's no use," the old man said. "Its skin is too strong. No mortal weapons harm it: not clubs, stones, spears, arrows or knives."

"Help me just the same."

PERSEPHONE

Virgo

It was getting dark, and Persephone's friends the wood-nymphs had all gone home. She alone had stayed in the fields beside the wood. She was helping a farmer to find one of his piglets. It had strayed from its mother and lost itself among the trees, looking for acorns.

"Ah, there you are," said Persephone at last. She dropped her flowers and ran to pick up the little pig. She took it back to its owner, and he set off cheerfully for home, driving the squealing pig-family in front of him.

Suddenly, just as he was out of sight among the trees, he heard Persephone screaming behind him. "Help! Help!" He ran back as fast as he could. He was just in time to see the whole field gape open, like a huge mouth opening to the Underworld. From the hole a chariot appeared, pulled by four night-black horses. As the terrified farmer watched, the chariot-driver snatched up Persephone under one arm, wheeled his horses round and galloped back into the dark ground. The hole closed behind them, and the field lay grassy and quiet again, as if it has never been disturbed.

The sound of Persephone's screaming had risen up to Olympos. It reached the ears of her mother Demeter, goddess of harvest and growing plants. She rushed down to earth to save her daughter. But she was too late. All she found in the field was the astonished pig-farmer, with his story of the ground opening and the nightmare charioteer.

"It was Hades," groaned Demeter. "The king of the Underworld has stolen Persephone. How can I ever get her back?"

She went to Zeus. But he refused to help. Persephone, in the Underworld, had eaten six pomegranate seeds – and anyone who eats the food of the Underworld must stay there forever.

Demeter was heart-broken. She refused ever to go back to Olympos, and banished herself to the coldest place she could find on earth. Here, dressed as an old beggar-woman, she sat by a barren rock and wept.

Time passed. Without Demeter, nothing at all could grow. All over the earth, plants withered and died. Farmland grew barren. Men starved. At last their wailing reached the ears of the gods in Olympos, and Zeus was forced to act. He called a council to decide what to do. How could be break Hades' power and bring Persephone back, when she had eaten the food of the Underworld?

At last it was decided. For each of the six seeds she had eaten, Persephone would have to live in the Underworld for one month each year. Those six months would be winter-time on earth, and all growing plants would sleep. For the other six months she could return to the earth, and at her coming, in Spring, Demeter would waken the plants and crops to life.

To show what he had decided, Zeus placed a new constellation in the sky, and called it The Maiden in honour of Persephone.

THE JUDGEMENT OF THEMIS

Libra

The scent of balsam filled the air and the whole forest held its breath, for a miracle was about to happen. Birds folded their wings and perched still on the branches; grasshoppers fell silent, and even the leaves on the trees stopped rustling in the breeze. In the stillness, the trunk of the balsam tree slowly, gently split open — and inside, snug in the hollow, lay a beautiful newborn baby boy. His name was Adonis, which means Prince.

The goddess Aphrodite was walking in the cool wood, gathering flowers. She heard the sound of a baby playing, and found Adonis lying happily on a bed of soft grass.

"Oh, you darling," she cried, gathering him in her arms. "Who'll take care of you and mother you?"

She sat on the grass to think. Then she leaned forward, pressed her lips close to the ground and whispered, "Persephone! Sister! Come up! Come up!"

The ground split apart, and a pathway opened from the Underworld. Queen Persephone herself appeared. As soon as she saw the baby, she too was charmed by his beauty.

"Will you help me look after him and bring him up?" said Aphrodite. "As he grows older, he'll be too much of a handful for one of us alone."

"Gladly," said Persephone.

For many years the two goddesses looked after Adonis in peace and happiness. For the six months of winter, while Persephone lived in the Underworld, he was in Aphrodite's charge; in spring, when Persephone returned to the earth, she took care of him until summer's end.

As Adonis grew older, and turned from a beautiful baby into an attractive boy and a handsome, princely young man, the two goddesses began to quarrel over him. Each of them wanted to keep him for the whole year, and was jealous of the other's six months. Their squabbling and arguing grew louder with every year that passed, until finally it disturbed all Olympos and reached the ears of Zeus himself.

"What *is* the matter?" he asked angrily. The two goddesses started to explain – but even their explanation turned into an argument. "Be quiet!" shouted Zeus. "Go to Themis, goddess of common sense. She's the only one to settle this."

So Aphrodite and Persephone told Themis their problem. She thought for a while and then said, "It's easy. Each year Adonis will spend four months with Aphrodite and four with Persephone. The other four months are his to decide: he can choose which one of you he wants."

Everyone agreed to this, and the quarrel was settled. In fact Adonis chose to spend his own four months with Aphrodite – but Persephone agreed that it was his free choice, and that it was fair.

ORION

This is how Orion was born. One day Zeus, Hermes and Poseidon, feeling bored, decided to leave Olympos for a day and go for a walk on earth.

Disguised as mortal travellers, they walked all day in the woods and fields, until they were footsore and hungry. They called at the house of a poor farmer, Hyrieus, and asked him to give them something to eat. Hyrieus was a kind and generous man. He made the travellers welcome, and because he had no other food in the house, he killed his only ox, a family pet, to make their evening meal.

After they'd eaten, the travellers revealed themselves as gods. "As a reward for your kindness," Zeus said to Hyrieus, "ask for any gift you like, and it will be yours."

"My lord," said Hyrieus, "the only gift I want in all the world is a son of my own. But how can that be? My wife has been dead and buried for many years."

Scorpio

"This is what you must do," said Zeus. "Take the ox-skin and bury it in your garden. After nine months it will turn into a handsome son." So saying, he touched the skin with his royal staff, and the three gods disappeared into the evening sky.

Hyrieus buried the ox-skin as he'd been told. For nine long months he waited impatiently – and then one day, standing on the spot where the skin had been, he found a newborn baby, and called him Orion.

Orion grew up strong and proud. He was a skilful hunter, and often used to go out into the countryside to look for game. When he was grown-up he left his father Hyrieus and set out to see the world. Wherever he went he was sure to go hunting in the local forests and mountain-sides, and his fame soon spread round all the world.

One day, while he was hunting on the island of Crete, he met Artemis the hunting-goddess herself. For days they hunted together, tracking the wild beasts of the hills and woods. Orion was so delighted with Artemis, and so proud of his own hunting skill that he decided to do something really unusual to surprise her. He went out alone one day, and that evening, when the goddess went to find him, he proudly showed her a huge heap of dead animals and birds. "There, Artemis!" he said. "In your honour, I've killed every living thing on Crete."

Unfortunately, Orion didn't know that Artemis, as well as being the goddess of hunting, was also the protector of all wild animals and birds. She looked at the pile of wasted bodies, and stamped her foot angrily on the ground. At once an enormous scorpion sprang up out of the earth. "Hunt *that*, Orion!" she said.

Orion lifted his bow. But he was too slow. The scorpion arched its venomous sting and killed him.

Artemis looked down at his body. "To hunt a few animals for sport is allowed," she said. "But to kill everything in sight is proud and foolish." And she set the scorpion among the stars, to remind men forever of the risks of pride.

CHEIRON

Sagittarius

Cheiron was the king of the centaurs, who were creatures half man, half horse. Like all centaurs, he was fond of hunting, and was well known for his skill with bow and arrows. But many centaurs were also fierce and wild, like untamed horses; and Cheiron was quiet and gentle, a friend to everyone. He knew much about medicine, and many wounded men, gods and animals came to him to be soothed and healed.

One day Cheiron was walking quietly on the hillside, gathering herbs for his potions and medicines. All at once, in the distance, he heard loud shouts and whinnying, and the noise of fighting and clattering hooves. At once he put his herbs down in a safe place beside a stone, and galloped off to see what the trouble was.

In a wild part of the mountain there was a gully of broken stones. Only a few tufts of grass and some scattered pine trees grew in such a high, bare place. In this gully, Cheiron found a battle raging, fierce as fire. Some wild mountain centaurs had come down from the hills and were attacking Cheiron's own son Pholos. Pholos had only one helper – but this was Herakles, and he was armed with his bow and magic arrows.

What had started the fight? Herakles had been visiting his friend Pholos, and after a day's hunting they'd sat down to dinner. Pholos opened a jar of his best wine – and its scent was so delicious that it attracted wild centaurs from far and wide. Now they were all fighting to the death. The centaurs were throwing rocks and sharpened pine branches; Pholos and Herakles were defending themselves with clubs.

As soon as he saw what was happening, Cheiron galloped into the middle of the fight to put a stop to it. Just at that moment Herakles set an arrow to his bow and fired. The arrow was meant for one of the wild centaurs; but Cheiron galloped right across its path and it wounded him in one foreleg. He crashed to the ground, snorting and whinnying with pain. At once all the wild centaurs turned tail and galloped away up the mountain.

Herakles and Pholos ran up to Cheiron. He lay twisting in agony on the rocky ground.

"Quickly, father!" said Pholos. "Tell me what herbs to bring, what medicines will heal your wound."

"None," groaned Cheiron. "The poison on Herakles' arrows comes from Hydra's blood. No medicine on earth can conquer that."

"Oh father," said Pholos. "Such a cruel wound – will you die of it?"

"No," said Cheiron, grinding his teeth with pain. "Long ago the gods gave me immortality. I can never be killed, or die. I must live on, and endure this agony, for evermore."

But Zeus, from up in Olympos, saw Cheiron's pain and decided to help him. He took him into heaven, and set him free of his injured body by turning him into a constellation of stars. So Cheiron lives on forever, still watching over men and helping them from up in heaven.

CONSTELLATIONS

Although the constellations have Greek or Latin names, many of the stars that make them up are named in Arabic. This is because star-maps were made by Arabian astronomers.

22 December – 19 January

The Goat
Capricorn

Fairly easy to find in the autumn sky, if you choose a moonless night. Four main stars:

1 Capricorni-Gredi
2 Capricorni-Dabih
3 Capricorni-Deneb Algiedi
4 Capricorni

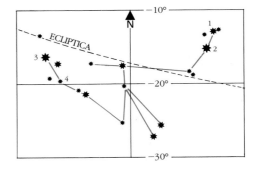

20 January – 18 February

The Water-carrier
Aquarius

Although its light is faint, this is one of the most beautiful constellations in the autumn sky. Four main stars:

1 Aquarii-Sadalmek
2 Aquarii-Sadalsud
3 Aquarii-Skat
4 Aquarii-Albali

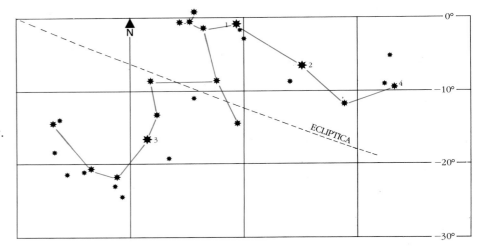

19 February – 20 March

The Fish
Pisces

Large and clear in the winter sky, this has two main stars:

1 Piscium-Alrisha
2 Piscium

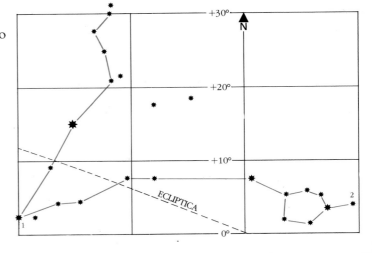

21 March – 19 April

The Ram
Aries

Hard to see, but sometimes visible in winter. Three main stars:

1 Arietis–Hamal
2 Arietis–Sheratan
3 Arietis–Mesarthim

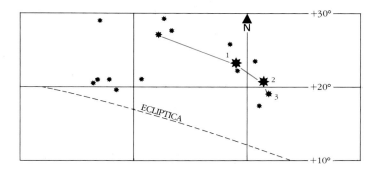

20 April – 20 May

The Bull
Taurus

Large and clear in winter. Two main stars:

1 Tauri–Aldebaran
2 Tauri–Nath

and two well-known groups of stars:

3 the Pleiades
4 the Hyades

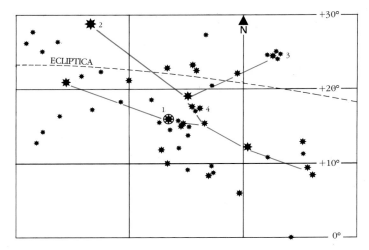

21 May – 21 June

The Twins
Gemini

This constellation is spread far out across the sky. Visible in spring. Two main stars:

1 Geminorum–Castor
2 Geminorum–Pollux

and two others of great brightness:

3 Geminorum–Alhena
4 Geminorum–Mebsuta

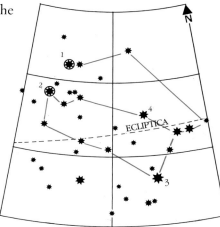

22 June – 22 July

The crab
Cancer

The hardest of all to see. Keep looking on spring nights, though: you may be lucky. Four main stars:

1 Cancri–Acubens
2 Cancri–Asellus Borealis
3 Cancri–Asellus Australis
4 Cancri

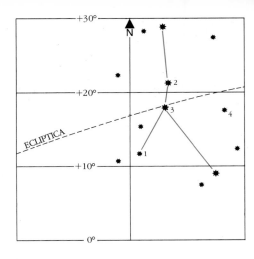

23 July – 22 August

The Lion
Leo

The brightest star in this constellation, Regulus (the king), glows like a blue diamond in the spring sky. Four main stars:

1 Leonis–Regulus
2 Leonis–Denebola
3 Leonis–Algieba
4 Leonis–Zosma

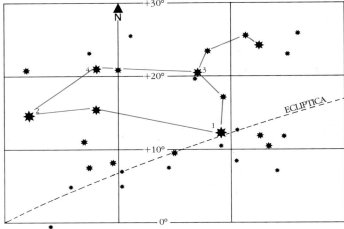

23 August – 22 September

The Maid
Virgo

One of the largest constellations in the summer sky. Four main stars:

1 Virginis–Spica
2 Virginis–Zavijah–Alaraph
3 Virginis–Porrima–Arich
4 Virginis–Vindemiatrix

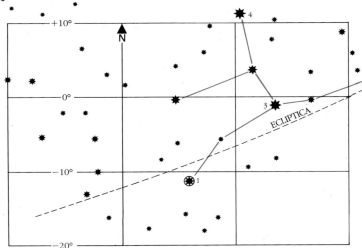

23 September – 23 October

The Scales
Libra

One of the fainter constellations in the summer sky. Four main stars:

1. Librae-Zuben-Elgenubi
2. Librae-Zuben Elschemali
3. Librae-Zuben Elakrab
4. Librae-Zuben Elakribi

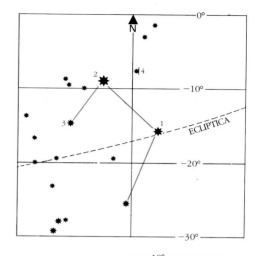

24 October – 21 November

The Scorpion
Scorpio

Of all the constellations, this one looks most like its name. You can easily make it out in the summer sky. Five main stars:

1. Scorpii-Antares
2. Scorpii-Acrab
3. Scorpii-Dschubba
4. Scorpii-Shaula
5. Scorpii

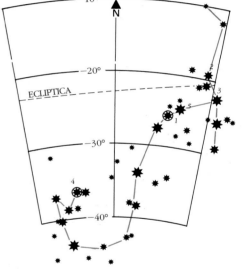

22 November – 21 December

The Archer
Sagittarius

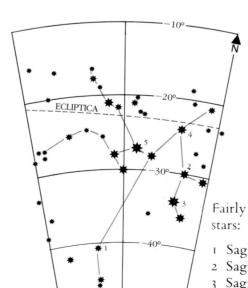

Fairly easy to see in autumn, this has five main stars:

1. Sagittarii-Alrami
2. Sagittarii-Kaus Medius
3. Sagittarii-Kaus Australis
4. Sagittarii-Kaus Borealis
5. Sagittarii-Nunki

WHAT IS A STAR?

A star is a ball of glowing gas which shines in the sky. Whether or not you can see a particular star from here on earth depends on (1) its size; (2) its temperature; (3) its distance from the earth, measured in "light years" (a light year is the distance light travels in a single year); (4) your position on the earth.

If you could walk on foot all the way from the earth to the moon – nearly 400,000 kilometres or 240,000 miles – it would take you ten years. But light travels from the moon to the earth in just over a second. (One light year equals nearly ten million million kilometres, or six million million miles.)

The stars are classed by brightness. Each class of star has a brightness about $2\frac{1}{2}$ times stronger or weaker than those in the next class. The lower the number, the brighter the stars.

| 6 | 5 | 4 | 3 | 2 | 1 | 0 |

WHAT IS A CONSTELLATION?

A constellation is a group of visible stars. To us they seem to form a particular shape, like that of a human being, an animal or an object.

Whether or not you can see a particular constellation depends on the time of year. Sun, moon and planets seem to travel across the sky on a path called the *ecliptic*; it's like an imaginary belt stretched round the sky. The band of sky each side of the ecliptic, called the *zodiac*, is divided into 12 equal sections. Most of the 12 sections (or "signs") of the zodiac were given their names more than 3000 years ago.

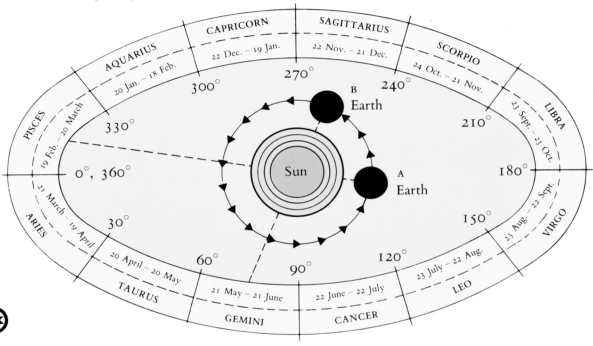

WHY DO THE CONSTELLATIONS SEEM TO CHANGE?

To us on earth, the sun seems to move across the background stars, and to pass from one constellation to another. Actually, the sun stays still and the earth revolves around it. But for us the effect is just the same. The constellations we can see change from season to season.

When the earth is at point A on the diagram the sun seems to us to be in the middle of the constellation Pisces. Three months later, when the earth has moved round to point B, the sun seems to have moved through Aries and Taurus and is now in Gemini. That's how the constellations seem to change.

To find the constellations in the sky above your own part of the world, you need to borrow from the library a good star-map or star-chart. Then check what you can see against what the book says should be there. The best time to look for constellations is just before midnight on a fine, cloudless night.

Good hunting!

Published by the Press Syndicate of the University of Cambridge
The Pitt Building, Trumpington Street, Cambridge CB2 1RP
40 West 20th Street, New York, NY 10011–4211, USA
10 Stamford Road, Oakleigh, Melbourne 3166, Australia

Originally published in French as *Quand Brillent Les Etoiles*
    by Editions Pierrot SA, Lausanne 1980
    and © Ghislaine Vautier and Jacqueline Bezencon 1980
First published in English by the Cambridge University Press 1981
    as *The Shining Stars*
English adaptations © Kenneth McLeish 1981
First paperback edition 1989; reprinted 1991

Printed in Hong Kong by Wing King Tong

ISBN 0 521 23886 2 hard covers
ISBN 0 521 37914 8 paperback